NEIL RICHARDSON

G000124928

Courting disaster

Should Christians and non-Christians
date each other?

DayOne

© Day One Publications 2005

First printed 2005

ISBN 1-84625-007-2

9 781846 250071 >

British Library Cataloguing in Publication Data available

Published by Day One Publications
Ryelands Road, Leominster, HR6 8NZ
☎ 01568 613 740 FAX 01568 611 473
email—sales@dayone.co.uk
web site—www.dayone.co.uk
North American—e-mail—sales@dayonebookstore.com
North American—web site—www.dayonebookstore.com

Designed by Steve Devane and printed by Gutenberg Press, Malta

Contents

This little book hits the nail on the head! If we are going to call ourselves Christians, then we should submit to the authority of God's holy Word, the Bible. The Bible makes it clear—Christians are to marry Christians! In Western Culture, people seem to 'date' as the primary means of finding a spouse. We usually marry people we date. The bottom line must be: Christians do not date or marry non-Christians. Someone has said: 'The three words in the mind of a bride are the aisle, altar, hymn or I'll alter him.' As Neil Richardson has elegantly and biblically defended, the Bible, not our emotions and feelings, must be our guide in these most important areas of life. I recommend this book for singles and parents alike!

Dr Jobe Martin, DMD, Th.M
Founder of Biblical Discipleship Ministries and author of *The Evolution of a Creationist* and originator of the video *What God says about relationships, marriage and family*

This book is a thoughtful, practical and—above all—passionate plea for wholehearted discipleship in an area of great relevance for all Christian young people and youth group leaders.

Christopher Ash

Christopher Ash is the director of the Cornhill Training Course and author of *Marriage: Sex in the Service of God*

Acknowledgements

Big thanks to Jo Jackson, Mirren Martin and Chris Hawthorne for proofreading and godly input.

Thanks to John Roberts, Jim Holmes, Roy Chapman and Suzanne Mitchell for their insightful suggestions and amendments.

Also, big grins to my little sister, Josephine (PhD!), who inspired me with the title and initial ideas.

This is dedicated to my beautiful fiancée, Yasmine.

There are many instances where I use examples and refer to a person who may be either male or female, so, in order to avoid repeatedly saying 'he/she' or 'him/her', I have alternated the use of 'he' and 'she' through the chapters.

Introducing the subject

Necessary attitudes

There is one purpose in life: 'to glorify God, and to enjoy him forever'.[1] The aim of this book, therefore, is to encourage us to please God by submitting our wills to his.

The Son of God says, 'If you love me, keep my commandments.'[2] If Jesus is to be our Saviour, he must also be our Master. This involves actions as well as words: 'Why do you call me "Lord, Lord", and not do the things which I say?'[3] It is impossible to love God while continuing to ignore his instructions: 'He who says, "I know him," and does not keep his commandments, is a liar, and the truth is not in him. But whoever keeps his word, truly the love of God is perfected in him. By this we know that we are in him. He who says he abides in him ought himself to walk just as he walked.'[4]

There are four things that are necessary if this book is to help us:

1. We have to want to please God

If you are interested *primarily* in having a happy life, having fun, justifying your behaviour or even being a good person, then this isn't for you. You really need to go and read the Gospels, to repent of your sins and to entrust your life to Jesus Christ. Then, it would be good to go and find a true Christian and explain to him or her what you have just done. Pray together with that person. Then perhaps come back and read this book! First things first—and the first thing for each of us is to get right with God. 'Without faith it is impossible to please [God].'[5]

2. We have to believe that the Bible is God's perfect and sufficient Word

This means that we must understand that the Bible is a book that stands *over* us. We do not stand in judgement on the Bible, but as Jesus says, 'He who rejects me, and does not receive my words, has that which judges him—the word that I have spoken will judge him in the last day.'[6] If we have a pick 'n' mix attitude to the Bible, accepting the bits we like and passing over the bits we don't like, we reject God's Holy Spirit who took the time to inspire 'all Scripture [which] is given by inspiration of God, and is profitable for doctrine, for reproof, for correction [and] for instruction in righteousness, that the man of God may be complete, thoroughly equipped for every good work.'[7] Notice the words 'all', 'thoroughly' and 'every'. The Bible is *sufficient*. We don't need any additional teaching to the Bible, we just need to discover what is written there and apply it to our lives with the help of God's Spirit. What I write here I seek to draw from the Bible. I ask you to 'test everything' I say,[8] not by your own emotions or experiences, but by the Bible. Please have a Bible with you at all times while reading this, so you can check that I am not making it up out of my own imagination! If I say something truly biblical, please do it. God will surely bless you. If I say something unbiblical, please let me know by contacting the publisher. Then I can change it in conformity to God's Word. Thank you in advance!

3. We have to believe that God has our best interests at heart

One of my favourite verses is Psalm 84:11 which says, 'For the LORD God is a sun and shield; the LORD will give grace and glory; no good thing will he withhold from those who walk uprightly.' Do you believe this? Can you grasp that God cares more about your well-being and eternal happiness than you do? Does it not make perfect sense, then, to obey God in every particular and let him give us what he thinks is best for us? How can we possibly know what is best for us? How can God not know? Do you want more evidence that God wants the best for us? Look at Jesus. 'Greater love has no one than this, than to lay down one's life for his friends.'⁹ 'He who did not spare his own Son, but delivered him up for us all—how shall he not with him also freely give us all things?'¹⁰ God himself was prepared to humble himself and come to this earth as a poor baby, and be crucified by those whom he created, to die for *us* and our sins. Don't you think God must care enough about *you* to give you everything else you need? If he gave you the best possible thing he could ever give—his Son's life—don't you think he will give you every other good thing as well? Jesus promises, 'I have come that [you] may have life, and ... have it more abundantly.'¹¹

4. We have to pray

I hope and pray that these words will be God's words, as well as mine. I ask you with all sincerity to put this book down before you read any further and pray to God. I confess that I often neglect to do this when I take up my Bible, and then I find it really heavy-going or impenetrable. This is unwise! I need God's Spirit to open up my mind and heart to receive the good news in his Word. Even David needed this: 'Open my eyes, that I may see wondrous things from your law.'¹² So stop right now and pray. With an undivided and sincere heart, ask God to show you the truth, and he will: 'When he, the Spirit of truth, has come, he will guide you into all truth.'¹³

STOP AND PRAY!

Why this is so important
Thank you for getting your Bible, praying and reading on. I'd like to fill

you in a little more on why I've come to write about this subject of *dating non-Christians*.

First, I'd like to define 'dating', or 'going out'. The Bible seems to expect human beings to fall into these categories: single (e.g. Paul[14]), engaged (e.g. Mary[15]), married (e.g. Peter[16]), widowed (e.g. Anna[17]) or divorced (1 Corinthians 7:15). There does not seem to be a 'going out' category. We seem to have invented this, perhaps partly to fit in with our twenty-first century Western culture which has people marrying much later and prioritizing education and career over and above family and community. People don't want commitment, but they do want intimacy, so they 'go out' or 'date'. This way, we get physical and emotional pleasure without having to dedicate our will and life to someone in a permanent partnership. It sounds great, but you only need one eye half-open to see what a mess we've made of it. It doesn't work. Without commitment, the pleasure attained from intimacy soon evaporates as mistrust, insecurity and infidelity seep in. Josh Harris has written an excellent book entitled *I Kissed Dating Goodbye* (Multnomah, 2003) which addresses this subject in an honest and greatly helpful fashion.

I'm not saying it's impossible to go out with someone in a godly way, but if we define 'going out' as commencing a romantic, intimate relationship with someone without any intention of committing to them permanently, then it's hard to see how that can please God. If we are to date someone, it must surely be with a view to finding out whether a lifelong commitment to each other, in God's service, is appropriate. It is *not* about seeing how far you can go sexually with someone until your conscience kicks in and you back off until the next time. If there is such a thing as 'going out', then the culmination of it is not physical intimacy but engagement. And the fulfilment of engagement is not physical intimacy but marriage. And the fulfilment of marriage is in honouring God together for life; a part of this is physical intimacy—the *final* icing on the cake.

Secondly, what is a 'non-Christian'? Well, the best way to define this is negatively. A non-Christian is someone who is not a Christian. What is a Christian? Let Christ himself define this: 'Most assuredly, I say to you, he who hears my word and believes in him who sent me has everlasting life, and shall not come into judgement, but has passed from death into life.'[18] A Christian, then, is someone who acknowledges Jesus in his or her *mind*: Christians believe in him. 'If you confess with your mouth the Lord Jesus and believe in your heart that God has raised him from the dead, you will be saved.'[19] Here we see that Christians are people who proclaim with their *mouths* that Jesus is Lord, and believe in Jesus (and his resurrection) in their *hearts*. Dramatically, a Christian is someone who has 'passed from death into life' and has 'everlasting life'. Jesus also says that 'no one can see the kingdom of God unless he is born again'.[20] We must have a brand new nature and be made new people if we are to cross over from death to life and enter into God's eternal kingdom. We cannot enter as we are—we 'who once were far off have been brought near by the blood of Christ'.[21] In short, non-Christians are those who have not personally acknowledged Jesus as Lord, nor believed on him in their hearts by faith.

The teaching explained in this book is this:

It is disobedient to God to be 'yoked' with a non-Christian.

I will go on to define carefully what it means to be 'yoked', and to argue that this certainly includes marriage and, by implication, dating, since dating is the prelude to engagement and marriage. I hope to convince you that there is no point to dating if it is not serious, and that it is disobedient to Jesus to get serious with someone who is not seriously committed to him.

First and foremost I aim to show you how the Bible clearly insists on this teaching, but I also have various personal reasons which drive me to write this at this time. Here are two of them:

1. Observation and experience

I committed my life to Jesus Christ when I was a small boy. I was baptized when I was thirteen and have since then often sought to give a public testimony to my beliefs. I've never had a problem with talking, but what I have failed to do, however, is love God and people enough to obey him. I thought I could have my cake and eat it—be a Christian but live like a non-Christian at the same time.

Slowly and painfully God had to show me a better way than the one I taught myself. I hope to share this way with you, so that you can *avoid* some of the classic mistakes we make. I praise the Lord that he will do whatever it takes to bring about our sanctification (separation from sin to himself—see 1 Thessalonians 4:3 and Romans 8:29).

So, even though I seek to be thoroughly biblical in what I say, I want you to know that I am also drawing from experience. I sympathize greatly with whatever struggle you or your friends may be going through. I certainly don't want you to feel that I am promoting myself as someone who has 'arrived' and now pleases God perfectly. I am a new creation by God's grace alone. Paul says, 'Do not be deceived. Neither fornicators, nor idolaters, nor adulterers, nor homosexuals, nor sodomites, nor thieves, nor covetous, nor drunkards, nor revilers, nor extortioners will inherit the kingdom of God. And such were some of you. But you were washed, you were sanctified, but you were justified in the name of the Lord Jesus and by the Spirit of our God.'[22]

I have also seen too many Christian friends fail. They have started to deceive themselves and those around them. They have 'made God out to be a liar'[23] and thought they could do what they felt like while still calling themselves disciples of Jesus. They have started going out with non-Christians.

Later on, I will discuss some of the reasons which motivate people to get involved in romantic relationships, and some of the justifications that are used for starting to see non-Christians in particular. At this point, though, what I want to make crystal clear is this: if I were the devil, one of the very greatest weapons I could use against any Christian would be to entice him into the arms of an unbeliever. There are very few methods more guaranteed to help us to fall away from God than the giving of our hearts to one of his enemies, even if they don't fully realize their opposition to God. Do you suppose that your heart can withstand such a clash of loyalties? Sooner or later you would have to give up one, and the sad testimony of many is this: those who leave it until later to choose between God and their non-Christian lover end up rejecting God and choosing the unbeliever. If you've read this far, I don't think you want that—praise God!

2. Love

This might sound a little pious, but I truly hope and pray that what moves me to write this is the love of God for his people. He loves to see us obeying him and living our lives in the light of his presence. We can't do that if we've set our faces against his law (which is another way of saying 'his character'). We can only experience the true joy and peace that God alone can give if we submit to his will in all things, especially in the matters of our hearts. I don't want you or anyone that you love to be in bondage to sin, and, as I've already said, this is one of the devil's favourite schemes to bring that about. Let God set you free as you trust his loving instruction and surrender to his will. 'But now having been set free from sin, and having become slaves of God, you have your fruit to holiness, and the end, everlasting life.'[24]

So now, please read on to find out what the Bible says about ...
- just exactly *why* it is wrong to go out with a non-Christian
- what our motives are and how we justify ourselves

- what the eternal consequences are of going out with a non-Christian
- some common objections
- what the positive alternatives are

STOP AND PRAY!

Notes

1 *The Westminster Shorter Catechism,* Question 1.

2 John 14:15.

3 Luke 6:46.

4 1 John 2:4–6.

5 Hebrews 11:6.

6 John 12:48.

7 2 Timothy 3:16–17.

8 1 Thessalonians 5:21 (NIV).

9 John 15:13.

10 Romans 8:32.

11 John 10:10.

12 Psalm 119:18.

13 John 16:13.

14 1 Corinthians 7:7.

15 Luke 1:27.

16 1 Corinthians 9:5.

17 Luke 2:37.

18 John 5:24.

19 Romans 10:9.

20 John 3:3.

21 Ephesians 2:13.

22 1 Corinthians 6:9–11.

Chapter 1

23 1 John 1:10 (NIV).
24 Romans 6:22.

Why is it wrong to date a non-Christian?

The Bible says NO to believers and unbelievers being joined together

I f you are a believer in Christ, it is wrong to date someone who is not (yet) a Christian because … *the Bible says we should not join together with unbelievers.* Since we believe the Bible to be God's perfect[1] Word to all his children, there can be no greater reason than this. Imagine a pair of scales. Now imagine, on one side, an infinite number of fine-sounding reasons for going out with someone. In your mind's eye, on the other side put *one single Bible verse* which says you should not do this. That single piece of God's pure and precious Word, which Jesus says 'cannot be broken',[2] that one verse will weigh down the scale-pan right to its base. Why? 'Because the foolishness of God is wiser than men.'[3]

It is completely assumed in the Bible that a Christian will only court or marry a fellow believer. This is why 1 Corinthians 7:39 says that a widow may remarry, but 'only in the Lord', and why Paul, speaking of his rights as an apostle, says that he has a right 'to take along a believing wife', literally 'a sister' or 'a spouse'.[4] This echoes Song of Solomon 5:1–2, in which the man speaks of 'my sister, my spouse'. Brothers and sisters in Christ should be the only people we consider going out with or marrying, and, even when we do marry a fellow believer, our *primary* relationship with them is *still* as with a brother or sister in Christ. This is the relationship which endures for eternity, although, of course, there is now a unique and unbreakable marital intimacy for the rest of this life.

But, as well as this, here is the *key passage* which explains why we should not go out with or marry unbelievers:

Do not be unequally yoked together with unbelievers. For what fellowship has righteousness with lawlessness? And what communion has light with darkness? And what accord has Christ with Belial? Or what part has a believer with an unbeliever? And what agreement has the temple of God with idols? For you are the temple of the living God. As God has said:

'I will dwell in them
And walk among them.
I will be their God,
And they shall be my people.'

Therefore

'Come out from among them
And be separate, says the Lord.
Do not touch what is unclean,
And I will receive you.
I will be a Father to you,
And you shall be my sons and daughters,
Says the LORD Almighty.' (2 Corinthians 6:14–18)

What can we learn from this?

1. Believers and unbelievers are unequally yoked (v. 14)

When two animals are ploughing a field or pulling a load, they are yoked together with a special piece of wood. As you can see from the picture on the next page,[5] the two oxen are extremely similar in breed, build and characteristics, even down to the black tips on the end of each horn. Because they are of equal height, the yoke fits neatly across their necks and shoulders, guiding them both to walk in the same direction. Labouring animals need yokes on them otherwise they wander off in all kinds of directions. As you can see in the picture, even equal animals with the same yoke find it hard to face in the same direction.

Jesus says, 'Take my yoke upon you and learn from me, for I am gentle and lowly of heart, and you will find rest for your souls. For my yoke is easy and my burden is light.'[6] The Bible argues that everyone has some kind of 'yoke' or guiding principle upon them.[7] Romans chapter 6 says that you are a 'slave to sin'[8] until Christ frees you from its 'dominion over you'.[9] As an unbeliever, you have been 'taken captive by [the devil] to do his will'.[10] But when Christ enters your life, he breaks the yoke of sin, death and the devil, and places his own yoke upon you. Even though we may think that following Jesus is difficult, with his power within us it can actually be easy and light in comparison with

the drudgery of a meaningless life of rebellion and sin. When we turn to Jesus, our love for him is a powerful motive to keep his commandments, and not find them burdensome,[11] as we did when we were still rebels.

Now it makes sense that, if we are seeking a partner for life's journey, we should look for someone who has this same yoke upon her, this same driving force within her—Christ's Spirit. Even two unbelievers can understand this. For example, 'during the height of the lesbian feminist movement of the seventies, even many heterosexual feminists refused to marry because they believed marriage to be an inherently patriarchal and oppressive institution'.[12] The driving force of feminism was powerful enough to subjugate one of their most basic instincts, heterosexual monogamy. These women put their principles (however misguided) above their natural desires. Hilary Clinton initially refused repeated requests from Bill to marry him because, despite being attracted to him, she was afraid she would be overwhelmed by his personality and that he saw her merely as a target on his list. F. Scott Fitzgerald's wife, Zelda, refused to marry him initially because he was too poor. He represented this in his famous novel, *The Great Gatsby*, in which the title character is turned down by Daisy for the same reason.

The point is this: it is obvious that if two people marry, they must have the same guiding principle in their lives. If a Christian female marries an atheist male, for instance, disaster awaits. The man believes that when you're gone, you're gone, and so will live 100 per cent for this life. The woman believes that this life on its own is 'vanity and grasping for the wind';[13] it is only the briefest possible prelude to an unthinkably glorious eternity for her, but to an unimaginably miserable eternity for him.[14] This Christian wife has three options:

• Live her life in great grief at her husband's destiny, being constantly torn between her love for him and her love for the God he denies.

- Stop loving her husband so that she stops feeling grief over his destiny.
- Stop believing in hell, or that God will send unbelievers there.

I urge you not to choose such a crushing yoke as this.[15]

2. Believers are righteous and in the light, unbelievers are lawless and in the dark (v. 14)

The book of 1 John says that 'sin is lawlessness'[16] and the Antichrist is defined as 'the lawless one'.[17] Jesus describes himself many times as 'the light of the world'[18] and explains why people avoid and hate him so much: 'this is the condemnation, that the light has come into the world, and men loved darkness rather than light, because their deeds were evil. For everyone practising evil hates the light and does not come to the light, lest his deeds should be exposed. But he who loves the truth comes to the light, that his deeds may be clearly seen, that they have been done in God.'[19] True believers know that they are *not* righteous in themselves, but that they have received 'the righteousness which is from God by faith'.[20] Old Testament believers had the same testimony: 'I will bear the indignation of the LORD, because I have sinned against him, until he pleads my case and executes justice for me. He will bring me forth to the light; I will see his righteousness.'[21] So we do not look down upon unbelievers because they are still in darkness, since that is where we once were.[22] But neither do we flirt with, go out with or marry them! No, indeed, we love them and show compassion upon them not by dating them, but by praying for them. Why do we think we are such a marvellous gift to a non-Christian that they need us to date them? If we care so much for them, why don't we pray for them instead, that they might receive the greatest gift of all, the one gift they desperately need, Jesus Christ and his righteousness? As a friend of mine put it, 'If only Christian youth would choose to believe in the power of prayer more—they so often believe that it is all up to them to get this person saved and thus they date.'

3. Believers are the temple of God, which belongs to Christ, and unbelievers are idolaters, following after Belial (vv. 15–16)

When someone becomes a Christian she is putting herself under new management. She is admitting that she has been bought with an infinite price (that of Jesus' blood) and that she now no longer belongs to herself, but to God: 'Do you not know that your body is the temple of the Holy Spirit who is in you, whom you have from God, and you are not your own?'[23] All the earth belongs to God, since he made it and will judge it, but we who belong to Christ are actually his special treasure.[24] Verse 16 of our passage says that God dwells in us (by his Spirit) and that we are his people. Therefore, we do not have—as the US Declaration of Independence puts it—an 'inalienable right … to life, liberty and the pursuit of happiness'. No, on the contrary, we are dead to ourselves, but alive to Christ;[25] we are freed from sin, but slaves of righteousness;[26] we do not have the 'right' to pursue our own happiness, but rather to live entirely for the glory of God.[27] We have the privilege of being able to pursue God's happiness in loving him, obeying him and bringing other men and women to know him as we do.[28] We do not have the right to get into a relationship as and when we feel like it. Our romantic relationships, like everything else in our lives, should be 'all to the glory of God'.[29] We belong to Christ, not to ourselves. And, wonderfully, he belongs to *us*, and is more dedicated to our present well-being and eternal joy than we could ever ask or think![30] We really can trust him with our love lives.

Verse 15 asks 'what accord [Christ has] with Belial'. The word for 'accord' in Greek is *sumphonesis*, from which we derive our word 'symphony'. 1960s avant-garde composer John Cage separated two conductors by a partition, then put them in charge of the same orchestra. The result was utter chaos. His concerts, called 'happenings', were often events of sheer noise and confusion, or simply silence. This is the kind of 'symphony' we create when we partner a believer with an unbeliever. They are both trying to play the same tune (marriage), but are following two totally different conductors (Christ and Belial). This is not so much symphony as cacophony. Or a terrible, alienated silence.

Now, who is this Belial? Well, as you might have guessed, it's another name for the devil, one which particularly emphasizes his wicked worthlessness. The word is used sixteen times in the Old Testament, nearly always in the form 'children of Belial'. The sons of Eli, for example, are described as 'sons of Belial; they did not know the LORD'.[31] So anyone who does not know God personally is a son of Belial. And what are the characteristics of a son of Belial? '"The sons of Belial have gone out from among you and enticed the inhabitants of their city, saying, 'Let us go and serve other gods'"—which you have not known.'[32] The main truth about unbelievers is that they avoid the true God and serve other gods, and also seek to entice others to worship idols along with them. This is a crucial point. Romans 1 makes it crystal clear that people deliberately 'suppress the truth' about God, truth that can be 'clearly seen' in creation. After doing this, they 'worship and serve the creature rather than the Creator'. This idolatry leads them to 'vile passions', 'a debased mind' and a whole host of sins including gossip, boasting, backbiting and disobedience to parents. Finally, they seek to drag others down with them by approving of similar behaviour in others,[33] even thinking 'it strange that [Christians] do not run with them in the same flood of dissipation, speaking evil of [them]'.[34]

These are extreme and shocking words, but they describe the natural outcomes of the unbelieving heart, the heart that has turned itself away from and hardened itself against its Creator. And just as a Christ-centred heart will inevitably seek to win others over to its Lord, so will a self-centred heart seek to draw others away from that same Lord.

Right from the beginning, Abraham was absolutely adamant that his servant should take an oath 'by the LORD, the God of heaven and the God of the earth, that you will not take a wife for my son from the daughters of the Canaanites, among whom I dwell'.35 You rarely find Abraham speaking this strongly. This is because he knew that if his son Isaac married a Canaanite woman, Isaac's relationship with the true God would be greatly jeopardized. Unfortunately, Isaac's son Esau didn't realize this, and he married not one but two Canaanite women, who 'were a grief of mind to Isaac and Rebekah'.36 Esau never found his way back to God 'for he found no place for repentance, though he sought it diligently with tears'.37 Instead, he tried to make amends by marrying yet another wife!38

Later, through Moses, God enshrined this principle of *no intermarriage with unbelievers* in the Law, 'for they will turn your sons away from following me, to serve other gods; so the anger of the LORD will be aroused against you and destroy you suddenly'.39 In God's mind it is quite clear: marrying an unbeliever leads to idolatry on the part of the believer, not faith on the part of the unbeliever. Through this first act of disobedience (intermarriage), the believer is already fatally compromised and so inevitably many other sinful compromises will follow. Joshua 23:13 says, 'Know for certain ... they shall be snares and traps to you, and scourges on your sides and thorns in your eyes, until you perish from this good land which the LORD your God has given you.' Imagine a chair representing godly living. If a believer is standing on this chair next to an unbeliever who is standing on the floor, rooted in this world and its values, with all its gravity and force, and they are both pulling at each other, who do you think will win this particular tug of war?

Throughout the Bible we have too many examples for comfort of children of the Lord who have made a shipwreck of their lives through being unequally yoked with children of Belial. Here are just three, each of which illustrates a different disastrous outcome from getting involved with unbelievers:

A. FLAGRANT IMMORALITY LEADING TO A PLAGUE (THE ISRAELITES AND THE MOABITES). You can read this sorry story in Numbers 25. As soon as the Israelites started mixing with the Moabite women (v. 1), they started bowing down to their gods as well (v. 2), until they ended up blatantly engaging in pagan revelry, right in front of Moses' (and God's) face. We should thank God that he doesn't choose to deal with us in the way that he dealt with that disobedience then. I'll leave you to look it up!

B. WISDOM TURNING TO FOLLY AND A KINGDOM SPLIT (SOLOMON). His is the classic, and most tragic, case. How could it be that King Solomon, who 'surpassed all the kings of the earth in riches and wisdom',[40] could end up building a special shrine to Molech, the abominable god of the Ammonites?[41] (See illustration on page 24.) What a terrible legacy to leave his dynasty. When we come to his descendant Manasseh, 250 years later, the kings of Judah are *still* destroying their own children by fire for the sake of a bronze statue with a cow's head.[42] The desperately solemn lesson we must learn from Solomon is this: no matter how wise and wealthy you are, you will risk ruining everything if you marry an unbeliever. 'But King Solomon loved many foreign women ... from the nations of whom the LORD had said to the children of Israel, "You shall not intermarry with them, nor they with you. Surely they will turn away your hearts after their gods." Solomon clung to these in love. And he had 700 wives, princesses, and 300 concubines; and his wives turned away his heart. For it was so, when Solomon was old, that his wives turned his heart after other gods; and his heart was not loyal to the LORD his God ... Solomon did evil in the sight of the LORD, and did not fully follow the LORD, as did his father David ... So the LORD became angry with Solomon, because his heart had turned from the LORD God of Israel, who had appeared to

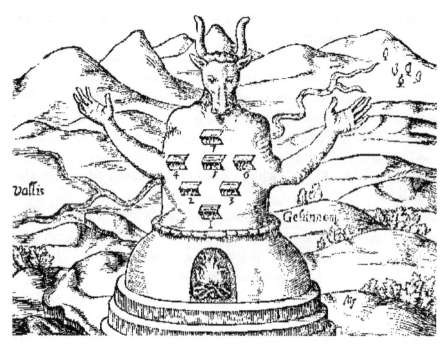

him twice, and had commanded him concerning this thing, that he should not go after other gods; but he did not keep what the LORD had commanded.'[43]

God consequently tore the kingdom away from Solomon, just as Solomon had torn himself away from the Lord who had so graciously given so much to him. It's a simple tragedy that Solomon clung to his wives more than he clung to God, causing strife, ruin and devastation not just for himself, but for his dynasty and for the whole Jewish race. Even though David married at least six women, God never rebuked him in such a severe way. David's major sins were adultery (Bathsheba), murder (Uriah) and pride (taking the census). God sent a plague upon 70,000 men as a result of this last sin, but continued to favour David and his dynasty. No, it was Solomon's turning aside after 'foreign' (idolatrous, non-Christian) women that ruined the nation, and led to idolatry and civil war and, ultimately, the total disappearance of ten whole tribes of Israel! If only Solomon, the wisest man of those times, had been wise enough to follow his own proverb, 'Do not give your strength to women, nor your ways to that which destroys kings.'[44]

C. DOGS RETURNING TO THEIR VOMIT (EZRA & NEHEMIAH'S MEN). Intermarriage with pagans led to idolatry. Idolatry led to murder and unrest, which led to the discipline of God upon Israel, which came in the form of exile to Assyria (northern tribes) and Babylon (southern tribes). God raised up Cyrus, a Persian king, to be 'his anointed'[45] and to pave the way for the Jews to return to their homeland, and by the time of Ezra (515 BC) the temple was rebuilt.

Amazingly, as soon as the people were back in the Promised Land, they leapt back into the arms of pagan women and men: 'The people of Israel and the priests and the Levites have not separated themselves from the peoples of the lands with respect to the abominations of the Canaanites ... For they have taken some of their daughters as wives for themselves and their sons, so that the holy seed is mixed with the peoples of those lands. Indeed, the hand of the leaders and rulers has been foremost in this unfaithfulness.'[46] When he heard this news, Ezra tore his shirt, his robe and some hair from his head and beard, and sat down astonished. How could this thing happen again so quickly? And the leaders were leading the way! They were living the proverb, 'As a dog returns to his own vomit, so a fool repeats his folly.'[47] Praise God that he gave the people Ezra, a man prepared to fall on his knees and cry out for his people and identify himself with them in their shame. He said that he was 'too ashamed and humiliated to lift up my face to you, my God; for our iniquities have risen higher than our heads, and our guilt has grown up to the heavens'. He continued by admitting that this particular area of disobedience had been the one that had led to the defeat and plunder of Israel time and again. He was grateful that God had 'punished us less than our iniquities deserve[d]' even before this point. All he could cry was, 'Here we are before you, in our guilt, though no one can stand before you because of this.'[48]

Oh that the Lord would raise up many Ezras in our time! If only we would take sin against our most holy God as seriously as this humble man did, even though he personally had not committed the sins. If only we would see how unfavourably God views getting yoked with unbelievers and how much grief it causes him and ought to cause us. God has delivered us, like the Israelites, out of the bondage of sin, and yet we happily throw ourselves back into that slavery.

The wonderful result for Israel was that, after the people had gathered round and seen the utter abandonment of Ezra's sorrow, the Lord moved them so that they too 'wept very bitterly'[49] and confessed their sins with a loud voice, and demonstrated the sincerity of their repentance by separating themselves from their pagan spouses.[50] And this is how we leave it at the end of the book of Ezra.

However, if you turn to the end of the next book, Nehemiah, you will see that exactly the same problem has arisen again! It seems unbelievable! Just as Jesus kept on going back to find his disciples sleeping when they should have been watching, so the children of Israel kept on joining themselves with idolaters. Their sinful nature was on autopilot. Unsurprisingly, Nehemiah is furious. He argues with them, pronounces curses upon them, hits a few of them, pulls out some of their hair and makes them swear by God to stop this wickedness once and for all! I don't know about you, but my immediate reaction is to say, 'Steady on! Don't you think you're being just a little bit harsh and unloving? Don't you think it would be better to bow down on your face like Ezra before the Lord, or at least to reason gently with these sinful men?' But I would be wrong. This man, Nehemiah, was an instrument of God and he was absolutely right.[51] This was the toughest kind of love he could show, but the men had demonstrated by their mulish repetition that it was the only language they would understand.

Nehemiah reminds them of Solomon, the greatest king in the world, who was beloved of God, but 'nevertheless pagan women caused even him to sin'.[52] This was his point: if the wisest man who had ever lived was ruined by sinful, foolish relationships, then we will be too.

There is an excellent song called 'The Exception' by Eddi Reader, in which she sings of a man who tries to buy his wife's affection only to find that she runs away with the milkman. The point of the song is that, even though he knew he was unwise and doomed to failure, he thought he might be the exception to the rule. And we all have a tendency to do this, to think that maybe we can bend the rules and that we will be the exception; that we will be the one man or woman who will actually remain completely untainted or unaffected by clinging to those who reject Jesus Christ and his wonderful love for them. Listen to the sound of your own voice if you ever start arguing like this: 'Oh but I'll never let that happen to me.' Remember Romans 12:3 and don't think more highly of yourself than you ought, 'but rather think of yourself with sober judgement' (NIV). And remember Solomon.

4. Believers must separate themselves from unbelievers if they want God to receive them as their Father (vv. 17–18)

I must first state clearly what these verses do *not* mean. They do not mean that we should run away and hide permanently in a monastery (or Bible college!) and never spend any time with non-Christians. God forbid—for how will they ever hear about Jesus without a preacher (yes, that means you, Christian!)?[53] Jesus says to his Father, 'I do not pray that you should take them out of the world, but that you should keep them from the evil one.'[54] In fact, you could say that there is no point being on this planet if we are never going to speak to a non-Christian. We are left here to fulfil the Great Commission (see the endings of Matthew, Mark and Luke, and the beginning of Acts) of bringing unbelievers to belief in Jesus! Thank the Lord that when you were a non-Christian someone spoke to you about Jesus so that you could repent, believe and be saved!

So what *do* these verses mean? Well, Jesus can help us again here. He is extremely direct about one central problem Christians often refuse to face up to: if you follow Jesus, you may well be hated as Jesus was. 'If the world hates you, you know that it hated me before it hated you.'[55] He goes on to explain that, as we now belong to him and are no longer of this world, this world hates us, even to the extent of thinking that if it kills us, it is doing God a service! If you read John's first epistle, you will see that most of it is about this contrast between 'the world' and God: 'Do not love the world or the things in the world. If anyone loves the world, the love of the Father is not in him.'[56] This letter is so full of love and tenderness (he keeps addressing his readers as 'beloved') but in that very lovingkindness John is absolutely black and white. The choice is: light or dark; God or the world/devil; love or hate. There is no 'both' or 'and'. There is no grey area or compromise. You see, you cannot have a foot in both camps with God. For his own glory and for my own benefit, he insists on having all of me, or none of me. It is the greatest insult to Jesus' sacrifice on Calvary if we say that we are prepared to give God all our lives except our 'love life'. He purchased every ounce of our souls. And if we don't like that, we are like the rich young ruler whom Jesus lovingly challenged—money or me? You can't worship both.[57]

So this is what it means to separate ourselves from unbelievers; not to ignore, avoid or be rude to them; not to have no friendship or camaraderie with them at all. How can we ever seek to win them for Christ if we are not *more* loving than their other non-Christian friends? No, biblical separation means behaving in an entirely different way from unbelievers while living and working in the same environment, and loving them with the compassion of Christ, not with the passion of our old natures. Jesus ate and drank with sinners, but he never got drunk. He loved prostitutes, but he never behaved improperly with one (I tremble to say such a thing). He dined with tax collectors but was so poor that he had to borrow a denarius for an illustration. Jesus is our ultimate example of godly separation from unbelievers. He only really separated himself physically from people when he had to go and pray alone to his Father (which happened often), and so we too need often to separate ourselves physically in order to pray alone in our rooms, with the door closed.[58] Apart from that, Jesus was available for whoever wanted to speak to him, from the Pharisees to Mary Magdalene.

This very Lord Jesus is the one we must 'put on ... and make no provision for the flesh, to fulfil its lusts'.[59] With the life and Spirit of Jesus himself within us, it is entirely possible to 'walk properly, as in the day, not in revelry and drunkenness, not in lewdness and lust, not in strife and envy',[60] unlike the unbelievers around us, while still showing them kindness and living peaceably with all men.[61]

As well as in our behaviour, we must separate ourselves from the attitudes and ambitions of unbelievers. Non-Christians fill their minds with the pleasures and cares of this life, building up houses and careers and families for themselves. We gaze back at the cross, the focus of our redemption, and yearn for the Second Coming of our Lord who will put all things right and reign over all. Unbelievers seek fortune, romance and power, or perhaps to make a name or feel good about themselves through charitable deeds or even religious practices. Our main ambition and aim should be entirely different: to 'preach the Gospel', especially 'not where Christ [is already] named',[62] that is, to those who have not yet had the opportunity to hear the good news, for the glory of God.

And the great promise at the end of all this 'sacrifice' on our part is that God himself will be a Father to us, and we will be his sons and daughters. Have you ever thought how utterly and completely you deserve to be destroyed by God? And now consider that he is willing to give you who believe the right to become a child of God![63] How is this possible? Because of one man, who once cried out, 'Eli, eli, lama sabachthani?' ('My God, my God, why have you forsaken me?').[64] So next time you think it a hardship to pass by an opportunity to date an unbeliever, think on your Lord, accursed by his Father, hanging there for you. Now, that's love, and *that's* the true sacrifice.

Notes

1 Psalm 19:7.

2 John 10:35.

3 1 Corinthians 1:25.

4 1 Corinthians 9:5.

5 Taken as recently as 1998!

6 Matthew 11:29–30.

7 Colossians 2:8.

8 Romans 6:6,16,17,20.

9 Romans 6:9,14.

10 2 Timothy 2:26.

11 1 John 5:3.

12 Stanley Kurtz, 'The Road to Polyamory', *The Weekly Standard,* 008/45, August 2003.

13 Ecclesiastes 1:14.

14 Matthew 25:46.

15 I should make clear that if a person becomes a Christian after marrying, then they should remain with their non-Christian partner as the Bible clearly instructs (1 Corinthians 7:10–16). Indeed, verse 16 of that passage gives a glimmer of hope to those who find themselves in such a predicament, and encourages them to persevere in loving, serving and praying for the unbelieving spouse. See also 1 Peter 3:1–2.

16 1 John 3:4.

17 2 Thessalonians 2:8.

18 1 John 8:12; 9:5; 12:46.

19 John 3:19–21.

20 Philippians 3:9; compare with Romans 10:6 and 2 Corinthians 5:21.

21 Micah 7:9.

22 1 Corinthians 6:11.

23 1 Corinthians 6:19.

24 Exodus 19:5.

25 Romans 6:11.

26 Romans 6:18.

27 1 Corinthians 10:31.

28 Colossians 1:28.

29 1 Corinthians 10:31; see Chapter 6 The positive alternatives.

30 Ephesians 3:20.

31 1 Samuel 2:12 (margin note).

32 Deuteronomy 13:13 (margin note).

33 Romans 1:18,20,25–26,28,32.

34 1 Peter 4:4.

35 Genesis 24:3.

36 Genesis 26:35.

37 Hebrews 12:17.

38 Genesis 28:6–9.

39 Deuteronomy 7:4.

40 1 Kings 10:23.

41 Molech was portrayed as a bronze statue, with a calf's head adorned with a royal crown, and seated on a throne. His arms were extended to receive the child victims sacrificed to him. Milton wrote that Molech was a frightening and terrible demon covered with mothers' tears and children's blood. Rabbis claim that, in the famous statue of Molech, there were seven kinds of cabinet. The first was for flour, the second for turtle doves, the third for a ewe, the fourth for a ram, the fifth for a calf, the sixth for an ox and the seventh for a child. When a child was sacrificed to Molech, a fire was lit inside the statue. The priests would then beat loudly on drums and other objects so that the cries would not be heard.

42 2 Chronicles 33:6.

43 1 Kings 11:1–10.

44 Proverbs 31:3. Although Proverbs 31:1 says that these are the words of the mother of King Lemuel, rabbis of old identified Lemuel with Solomon.

45 Isaiah 45:1.

46 Ezra 9:1–2 (margin note).

47 Proverbs 26:11.

48 Ezra 9:6,13,15.

49 Ezra 10:1.

50 The New Testament says that people who come to Christ while already married should remain married to their unbelieving partners, if the unbeliever wishes it. But it remains the case that a single Christian should not enter into a relationship with an unbeliever.

51 I am not necessarily recommending these tactics in seeking to restore a Christian! See Galatians 6:1–2.

52 Nehemiah 13:26.

53 Romans 10:14.

54 John 17:15.

55 John 15:18.

56 1 John 2:15.

57 Mark 10:17–22.

58 Matthew 6:6.

59 Romans 13:14.

60 Romans 13:13.

61 Romans 12:18,20.

62 Romans 15:20.

63 John 1:12.

64 Matthew 27:46.

What are our motives, and how do we justify ourselves?

You may have noticed that I gave only one main reason why it is wrong to date or go out with non-Christians: the Bible says NO to anything that links us up romantically with unbelievers. If that's not reason enough for you, nothing else I say will convince you. The Word of God is far more powerful than human reason[1] and if you love the Word-made-flesh (Jesus), you should want to obey the Word-on-paper (the Bible).

However, it may be useful to say a few brief words about what motivates us to want to go out with non-Christians.

Dating for fun?

Well, why do we want to date anyone? As I've said in Chapter 1, dating or courtship or going out should be with a view to getting engaged, which in turn should lead to marriage, God permitting. So we ought always to have firmly in mind the question: Could and should I spend the rest of my life with this person, living with them, sharing my money with them and probably raising a family with them? It might be hard for younger Christians to accept this, because they might think, 'All I want right now is a bit of fun'; however, that attitude is naïve for three reasons:

1. It leads to heartache

One person always takes things more seriously than the other when both start out 'just for fun'; the result is inevitable heartache. 'Like a madman who throws firebrands, arrows, and death, is the man who deceives his neighbour [girlfriend, boyfriend], and says, "I was only joking!"'[2] 'And in this matter no one should wrong his brother [or sister] or take advantage of him.'[3]

2. It is heading away from making God's kingdom our priority

The Christian life, as I've said, is not about the pursuit of fun. God is so kind that he makes quite a lot of it fun, but our concern is to 'Seek first the kingdom of God and his righteousness, and all these things shall be added to you'.[4] It really is incredibly enjoyable and pleasant to do the will of God once we have got over the initial reluctance that the flesh (our old nature) always tries to hem us in with. 'I delight to do your will, O my God, and your law is within my heart.'[5] What could be more pleasurable than knowing that we have pleased Jesus, the lover of our souls? What will count for more on Judgement Day and for the rest of eternity? And most Christians know this verse, 'Delight yourself also in the LORD, and he shall give you the desires of your heart.'[6] But please don't misunderstand: this does not mean that if you have an extended praise session in your living room, when you go outside God will have parked a Ferrari by your house with a beautiful woman or handsome man in it, all for you. Rather, it means that if you fill your mind with the things of God and his Word, God will give you what he has promised to give you: forgiveness,[7] eternal life,[8] all his riches in Christ,[9] everything you need for life and godliness,[10] joy inexpressible,[11] abundant life,[12] living water within you,[13] pleasures evermore at his right hand[14] and, most of all, himself.[15] Don't play with someone else's heart. Search after the Lord, and trust him to give you the right person to love seriously when he pleases and for his glory. Here is a simple question to ask yourself: would dating this person bring glory to God, be obedient to him, be an act of faith and be consistent with the pursuit of righteousness and his kingdom? Ninety-nine times out of a hundred you will know the answer.

3. It harms future relationships

Even if it seems like a bit of fun now, not serious or harmful, what you do now can drastically affect the happiness of your future relationships, particularly the one with the person you marry. I don't believe there is anyone reading this who would prefer their future husband or wife to have had many previous partners. It invites unhelpful comparisons and causes immense unnecessary confusion which can even jeopardize the relationship altogether. You may think your dating-for-fun is nothing, as light as the breeze. But Hosea 8:7 says, 'They sow the wind and reap the whirlwind.' What you think now is light and airy and pleasant and meaningless may end up being a tornado which threatens to wreck your marriage prospects.

Evangelistic dating?

It might be that you have genuinely found a person who seems perfect for you in every way. He really likes you, is friendly, not moody, kind, intelligent, funny, really attractive, fun, generous, unselfish, not possessive, wants the same number of children, has his own car, likes your favourite CDs, etc. The only 'little snag' is that he is not a Christian. Oh, but it's so frustrating! He's so much nicer than all of the *Christian* boys that you know! He is even willing to come to church sometimes if you ask him nicely. Maybe if you went out with him for a bit you could persuade him to give his life to Jesus? You can't bear to let him go, because someone else will surely snap him up, and you'll spend the rest of your life wondering, 'If only ...' So what you are beginning to say to yourself is, 'Yes, I could marry him. I really could. I'm not messing about. If only he was a Christian ...' But:

1. It pleases the devil

The thing to remember now is that you have an enemy. And the most important thing to remember about him is that he is incredibly subtle: 'Satan himself transforms himself into an angel of light.'[16] 'Angel' means messenger, and it may even *feel* as if God himself is giving you the message to date this non-Christian. It all seems so smooth, so natural, with so many events working together to bring this person into your life. Surely it must be right?

2. It pours scorn on the Bible

The devil is very happy for us to make decisions based on coincidences, impressions, feelings, events happening around us, advice from non-Christian or even Christian friends, and even 'spiritual' experiences as long as we don't obey the Bible: 'How can a young man cleanse his way? By taking heed according to your word.'[17]

When I was at university I lived in a shared student house. One young lady lived there for a little while and she was a lively, bubbly individual who attended the Charismatic Anglican church in London, Holy Trinity Brompton.[18] She explained to me that she had had a word from the Lord that she should go out with and probably marry a non-Christian young man she liked. I replied that God would never go against his revealed Word, the Bible, and showed her the key verses. She said that, no, she had prayed about it with others at her church, and 'had a peace from God in her heart' that she was doing the right thing. Needless to say, she and countless others from that time ended up on the scrap heap of faith, having entirely abandoned the Lord Jesus Christ because their feet had never been planted firmly on the solid rock of his Word. They had heard the Word of God, but, not wise enough to obey it,[19] had chosen rather to follow the imaginations of their hearts, calling them 'words', 'prophecies' or 'pictures' from the Lord. 'They speak a vision of their own heart, not from the mouth of the LORD.'[20] Obviously I'm not saying that God has never spoken in these ways, but that now we have God's perfect Word in all its fullness, the Bible is our only infallible guide, and must be the benchmark by which we test all these things (see 1 Thessalonians 5:21).

3. It places both of you in danger

Perhaps you feel that you are more sensible than this girl. You have no intention of going that far. Your plan is to date the person you like, but at the very beginning you aim to lay down a few ground rules, such as 'No getting physical before marriage' and 'No marriage until he becomes a Christian', and so on. You hope that by going out with him you can gradually begin to influence him for good and win him over to the Lord Jesus Christ through the power of your godly living and the kindness of your nature.

We have already reminded ourselves above, however, of the 'chair-gravity' principle. The person seeking to live for himself will *without fail* have a downward pull on the person seeking to live for Jesus, no matter how 'good' the Christian's intentions are. It works like this: when you are a single Christian, you have a war going on inside you. Galatians 5 calls this the war between the flesh and the Spirit. As a non-Christian, you did not have the Spirit of God,[21] so you had less of a struggle. You were made in the image of God, you had a conscience and the laws of society and various positive influences, but essentially you enjoyed sin and did not have the desire to please God. When the Holy Spirit awakened you and you came to your senses, repented of your sin and turned to Jesus, you received a new nature in Christ.[22] And so now your old, carnal, fleshly nature fights against your new, spiritual, God-pleasing nature (see also Romans 7). The battle lines are drawn up something like this:

The Holy Spirit	*vs*	*The devil*
The Word of God		*The world (in rebellion against its Creator)*
Conscience		*The flesh (sinful nature)*

As you can see, the unbeliever is outgunned because he or she has neither the Holy Spirit nor the Word of God. Hence all non-Christians, dramatic as it may sound, 'have been taken captive by [the devil] to do his will'.[23] When you became a Christian, suddenly the tables were turned. The devil is absolutely no match for the Holy Spirit, who is God. If you keep the Word of God hidden in your heart, the Bible says, you will not sin against God,[24] and you will be 'complete, thoroughly equipped for every good work'.[25]

However, a Christian who dates a non-Christian has, *from the very moment of embarking on the relationship*, turned the tables back in the enemy's favour again. The battle lines now look like this:

The Holy Spirit	*vs*	*The devil*
~~*The Word of God*~~		*The world (in rebellion against its Creator)*
~~*Conscience*~~		*The flesh (sinful nature)*
		Human reasoning
		Your new love (at war with your first love, God)

In order to let your human reasoning ('Maybe if I go out with him, he'll become a Christian.') triumph over the Word of God ('Can two walk together, unless they are agreed?'[26]), you have to effectively close your Bible and cross a line through it in your mind. Of course, you may still read it and refer to it for comfort from time to time, but as *the effective, decision-controlling authority* in your life, the Bible has been nullified by your disobedience. And if you are a true believer you will know that this is unacceptable, and your conscience will be stinging because you are grieving the Holy Spirit.[27] So, in order to have any 'peace', you will have to draw a line through your conscience, too. Praise God that, nevertheless, he never leaves us as orphans,[28] and that the Holy Spirit never leaves any true believer. But he may be grieved and choose to distance himself from us for a while because of our temporary rebellion. I say 'temporary' because the Bible says that no genuine Christian can ultimately lose his or her salvation,[29] but our temporary rebellions as Christians can go on for years and they *always have eternal consequences both for ourselves and for the non-Christians around us.*

Notes

1 Hebrews 4:12.

2 Proverbs 26:18–19.

3 1 Thessalonians 4:6 (NIV).

4 Matthew 6:33.

5 Psalm 40:8.

6 Psalm 37:4.

7 1 John 1:9.

8 John 5:24.

9 Philippians 4:19.

10 2 Peter 1:3.

11 1 Peter 1:8.

12 John 10:10.

13 John 4:14.

14 Psalm 16:11; who is at the right hand of the Father? Jesus! Jesus is our eternal pleasure.

15 Psalm 16:5.

16 2 Corinthians 11:14.

17 Psalm 119:9.

18 This was during the time of the 'Toronto Blessing' of the 1990s; HTB was at the heart of this in the UK.

19 Matthew 7:24.

20 Jeremiah 23:16.

21 Romans 8:9.

22 2 Corinthians 5:17.

23 2 Timothy 2:26.

24 Psalm 119:11.

25 2 Timothy 3:17.

26 Amos 3:3.

27 Ephesians 4:30.

28 John 14:18.

29 John 10:28. The Bible does teach, however, that there will be many 'professing Christians' (i.e. Christians in name only) who, although they show signs of faith, will fall away permanently at some point, because Jesus had never truly known them (Matthew 7:21–23; 13:1–23). If you are not sure whether you are a true believer in Jesus, read 1 John, and ask to pray with a trustworthy Christian.

The eternal consequences of dating a non-Christian

For the Christian

1. Our works will be burnt up and we will suffer loss

G iven that the Bible teaches 'eternal security',[1] it may surprise you that I say that there are eternal consequences for you, if, as a believer, you enter into such a relationship with a non-Christian. Temporary consequences include a deep-seated hollowness as the very author and perfecter of your life and faith (the Lord Jesus Christ)[2] is denied by the very essence of your outward lifestyle (dating someone who doesn't love him). Aside from the romantic thrill a relationship provides, Christian things will start to feel far-off and unreal, and church, Bible-reading and meeting with other Christians will seem false and undesirable. Times spent alone with the Lord will be virtually non-existent, because these give the Holy Spirit, the Word of God and your conscience an open goal, and you know that they will bring enormous conviction of sin upon your heart if given the chance. But perhaps you don't realize that there are everlasting ramifications for your choice.

The Bible says in 1 Corinthians 3:12–17 that all Christians build upon the foundation of their lives—that is, Jesus Christ. And nothing can shake that foundation. However, the things that are built on the foundation vary: some works are like gold, silver or precious stones, but others are far less valuable, like wood, hay or straw. The passage says very clearly that some work endures and some is burnt up. 'Each one's work will become clear; for the Day will declare it, because it will be revealed by fire; and the fire will test each one's work, of what sort it is.' And 'if anyone's work is burned, he will suffer loss; but he himself will be saved, yet so as through fire. Do you not know that you are the temple of God and that the Spirit of God dwells in you? If anyone defiles the temple of God, God will destroy him.3 For the temple of God is holy, which temple you are.' Incredible verses!

Let me apply this a little. You can see that Paul uses the 'temple of God' image once again to describe the believer, especially the believer's body.4 You can see how desperately important it is not to defile this temple. And he is saying that some Christians, although undoubtedly saved, will have virtually nothing to show for themselves other than that salvation on the Day of the Lord, when Jesus comes back. You see, it really does matter what kind of life we lead after we have knelt at the foot of the cross and asked Jesus to take our sins away. He has promised that he will do this and we will never fall into judgement for any sin we commit.5 But we *will* be judged for the good works we do as Christians, as to how genuine and pleasing to God they are. Some of our good works may be done out of greed, envy or pride, or half-heartedly, or through routine, or to impress others. Or maybe, like the people spoken of in Isaiah 1 and Amos 5, our good works are done as a substitute for repenting of hidden sins we are clinging on to, such as dating an unbeliever. The judgement seat of Christ will make all of this clear, and many such works will be burnt up because they simply are not pleasing to God. Only the good works done with 'clean hands and a pure heart'6 and out of a sincere desire to please God and love our brothers will endure and be rewarded. What a deeply sobering thought! 'The LORD is in his holy temple; the LORD is on his heavenly throne. He observes the sons of men; his eyes examine them.'7 This may seem a long way off, but we know from the Scriptures that Jesus' return is imminent:

it may be sooner than we think, like a thief in the night. We need to watch and pray, and be ready.

2. The blood of the unbeliever will be on our hands

It may sound as if I am deliberately trying to use shock tactics to stop you dating an unbeliever, but actually I'm probably not going far enough. It's virtually impossible to overstate the significance of our dealings towards non-Christians. This is why the children of Israel were punished by God so much, because they were supposed to be a light to the Gentiles but instead ended up causing the nations to blaspheme God because of their idolatry and waywardness.[8]

Ezekiel says early on in his book that, as a believer in the true God, he was a watchman to those who were not believers. The job of a man in a watchtower is to cry out to those who are down below, those who cannot see the dangers he can see. Now, when you are going out with a non-Christian, you can see things she cannot see. You understand that Jesus is alive, that he is coming again to judge the living and the dead[9] and that anyone whose name is not found in his Book of Life will be thrown into the lake of fire.[10] Unbelievers do not see this. They either think that when they're dead, that's it and there's nothing more, or that they're pretty decent people and they'll go somewhere a bit like here but nicer (but without God as they'd prefer to carry on ignoring him). They have no idea what horror awaits them, but you do. God says, 'I have made you a watchman ... therefore hear a word from my mouth, and give them warning from me: When I say to the wicked, 'You shall surely die,' and you give him no warning, nor speak to warn the wicked from his wicked way, to save his life, that same wicked man shall die in his iniquity; but his blood I will require at your hand.'[11]

A major problem in going out with an unbeliever is that your passion for her actually neutralizes your *com*passion for her. You so much want her to like you that you suppress the truth which you know she needs to hear (but won't want to), namely that she must repent and turn to Jesus. Or maybe you do half-heartedly tell her about Jesus, but the very fact that you are compromising your relationship with Christ by going out with her is like a big loud megaphone telling her that Jesus is not really all that important.

So essentially your self-love in wanting a relationship muzzles your genuine Christian love for a dying sinner, and, aside from other gracious interventions by God, she remains untouched by the gospel, and ends up in hell. Her blood is on your hands.

For the unchallenged and unrepentant non-Christian—the danger of perishing in sin and going to hell

The romantic moments that unbelievers have spent with Christians must, in their view, be something pretty special to make going to hell a price worth paying. And yet the unbeliever does not realize that if she does not repent this is likely to be the price she pays by going out with you, among other things. She cannot see what is going on in the spiritual realm: as the devil is undermining your confidence in God's Word and causing you to sin, he is also undermining any inkling of interest she may have in the things of God because she is watching you ever so closely to see whether your faith is something living, real, supernatural and totally life-defining, or just a hobby you do on Sundays while she stays at home and watches TV. Going out with her tells her your faith is just a hobby.

Put simply, if you love her, let her go. Put enough space between you and the unbeliever for her still to be able to see the Lord Jesus Christ and not be so overwhelmed by you and your confusing mixed messages. 'Cast your bread upon the waters, for you will find it after many days.'[12] 'Perhaps he departed for a while for this purpose, that you might receive him forever, no longer as a slave but more than a slave—a beloved brother.'[13] I personally recommend not having anything to do with a non-Christian to whom you are strongly attracted—no contact, no phone calls, emails, text messages, no dwelling on her in your mind. Leave her to the Lord. This requires a lot of trust in God—not taking things into your own hands but believing that he loves her more than you do and will reward your obedience.

It should be every Christian's utmost desire, like Paul, to want to see 'every man perfect in Christ Jesus. To this end I also labour, striving according to his working which works in me mightily.'[14] Paul, a single man, had truly grasped the secret of contentment—putting God's kingdom first and seeking the *eternal* welfare of those around him, not his or even their immediate happiness. And so your main desire for every non-Christian around you, whether you find them really attractive or very annoying, should be first and foremost to see them become your brothers and sisters in Christ[15] rather than anything else. If you don't have this wise desire, ask God, 'who gives to all liberally and without reproach, and it will be given to [you].'[16]

Notes

1 Also known as 'once-saved-always-saved' or 'the perseverance of the saints'.

2 Hebrews 12:2.

3 I think this can be compared to 1 Corinthians 5:5: 'deliver such a one to Satan for the destruction of the flesh, that his spirit may be saved in the day of the Lord Jesus.' In other words, the person who compromises for the whole of life in matters of sex and relationships, will, although a Christian, see her body (i.e. earthly life) and most if not all of her good works destroyed. Only her spirit will be saved, and nothing will be 'carried over' into heaven. There will be no crowns to cast at Jesus' feet, as described in Revelation 4:10.

4 Compare with 1 Corinthians 6:19.

5 Romans 8:1.

6 Psalm 24:4.

Chapter 4

7 Psalm 11:4 (NIV).

8 Ezekiel 36:20–23.

9 2 Timothy 4:1.

10 Revelation 20:15.

11 Ezekiel 3:17–18; compare with 33:6–7.

12 Ecclesiastes 11:1.

13 Philemon 15–16.

14 Colossians 1:28–29.

15 Song of Solomon 4:9–10. Note the placing of 'sister' ahead of 'spouse'.

16 James 1:5.

Some common objections

'I know a Christian couple and one of them wasn't a Christian when they first started going out.'

I, too, know one or two couples in this situation, but let me say these three things:

1. It is extremely rare

The chances of resisting being pulled off a chair by someone on the ground, even by someone much weaker than you, are incredibly slim. In the same way, for the tiny scrap of paper naming one or two examples where it worked out, there is a bulging case file in any mature Christian's life of fellow believers who have walked away from God through going out with and marrying a non-Christian or even a non-committed Christian.

2. God is gracious, but this does not mean we should sin[1]

Just because God has been kind to some disobedient Christians and brought good out of evil, this does not mean we should follow their pattern of behaviour. Just because David ended up taking Bathsheba as a wife and producing Solomon with her, it does not mean he would have recommended adultery and murder. Far from it. Even though his marriage seemed to work, the family was later troubled by big problems.[2]

3. Follow their advice, not their example

It would surprise me if these Christians would recommend the course of action they took, whether they were the person who was backsliding at the time or the one who was an unbeliever. Like people who have emerged alive from a crocodile-infested swamp, they would say, 'Thank God that we made it, but don't try it our way.'

'This kind of stuff isn't relevant to me. I'm too young/old.'

No you're not. If you're single, whether you're twelve or eighty-two, it is *always* worth 'purposing in your heart' beforehand, as Daniel did,[3] what you are going to do when the time of testing draws near. Are you going to buckle at the knees the first time an attractive, pleasant, 'open-minded' unbeliever comes near? Or are you going to be ready, having utterly dedicated yourself to God and his kingdom, determined to let him have the first say in the person you are going to spend the rest of your earthly life with, in his service, and to his praise and glory?

'Going out isn't the same as marriage. I'd never marry an unbeliever.'

I've addressed this pretty thoroughly in Chapter 2. Suffice it to say that if going out isn't preparation for marriage, then what is it for? Such aimless, faithless acts can never be pleasing to God or helpful for the other person.[4]

'I've been waiting for ages and I've never met a nice Christian boy/girl. There's no one suitable at my church. Maybe I'll never find a suitable Christian.'

It can be very frustrating for a believer to be told to marry 'only in the Lord',[5] when there are perhaps only two or three eligible singles in the whole church. Sometimes the temptation to move to another church just to broaden the pool of potential marriage partners can be quite strong, but it must be resisted if it means compromising on good Bible teaching or dropping existing friends and responsibilities which the Lord has given you: 'Let each one of you remain in the same calling in which he was called.'[6]

In addition to this, some kindly folk in churches are keen to see singles get married, partly because of the blessing that marriage has been to them, and partly because they are concerned about all the immorality, even in the church. So sometimes tacit or direct pressure can be put on the singles to marry each other, even if they are not really suited. Being in the same congregation ought not to lead automatically to being in the same marriage! So if you are already married and are 'looking out' for single friends, be prudent and remember that the Lord has different means of dealing with all of us, and that what has worked for you will not necessarily be right for another.

Here, then, we have a perceived problem: 'singleness'. And we have a perceived solution: 'marry someone in the next pew'. But singleness is not a problem; rather it is a genuine blessing, enjoyed by nearly everyone for at least twenty years of their lives, if you think about it. And the 'solution' is not to 'grab a believer before someone else snaps them up'. Neither is it to go to another church playing 'hunt the spouse'; nor is it to chase after an unbeliever.

What counsel remains, then, for the single believer who would quite like to be married, is in a small church with no one suitable, is getting pressure from married friends and is tempted to go to another church or date an unbeliever? Well, just because you can't find an item of clothing that you like in your size in the shop, does this mean you buy something ill-fitting and unsuitable? No. So with this situation; instead, you trust God and seek his counsel, patience and timing. 'The secret of the LORD is with those who fear him, and he will show them his covenant';[7] 'Oh, taste and see that the LORD is good; blessed is the man who trusts in him!... Those who seek the LORD shall not lack any good thing.'[8] It is better to wait for the Lord to find you the perfect fit, than to spend the rest of your life going about with the wrong thing! The Lord loves you so much: 'He who did not spare his own Son, but delivered him up for us all, how shall he not with him also freely give us all things?'[9]

'God has told me they're "the one"!'

Again, I have dealt with this in Chapter 2. Just remember that we are very, very talented at convincing ourselves that our preferences happen to be the same as God's will. Never forget the deceitfulness of your own heart, and trust God's Word only. [10]

If you have any more objections or suggestions like these, I would be delighted if you could let me know by contacting the publisher. Then I can continue to improve this book and make it as helpful as possible for my brothers and sisters in Christ.

Notes

1 Romans 6:1.

2 Psalm 51; end of 2 Samuel.

3 Daniel 1:8.

4 Romans 14:23.

5 1 Corinthians 7:39.

6 1 Corinthians 7:20.

7 Psalm 25:14.

8 Psalm 34:8,10.

9 Romans 8:32.

10 Jeremiah 17:5,9; Proverbs 28:26.

The positive alternatives

P rinciples for godly relationships leading to marriage are dealt with more fully in other books such as *Boy Meets Girl* (Multnomah, 2000) by Josh Harris, but here are a few biblical pointers.

Commit your works to the Lord, and your thoughts will be established[1]

Proverbs 16 is a wonderful 'guidance' chapter. It corrects any wrong thinking we may have about God being anywhere other than firmly on the throne of the universe, in charge of every little detail of our lives. What is interesting about verse 3 is the way in which the word 'thoughts' is used. Often we are about to embark on a course of action such as a relationship ('works') before we have even properly considered it ('thoughts'). The benefit in taking time to stop and commit every detail of our lives into the Lord's hands comes from the fact that it gives him time to sort out our thinking and thereby perfect the works we are about to do, to his glory. We may well end up doing the same thing we had planned to do, but the difference is that our *thoughts* will be established on him, and his glory, rather than on ourselves and our pleasures. Because the motive is entirely different, so will be the outcome. If this is not noticeable in this life, then it certainly will be in eternity: 'Well done, good and faithful servant; you were faithful over a few things, I will make you ruler over many things. Enter into the joy of your lord.'[2]

Be prepared to accept that God knows better than you do

If you are currently single, then God evidently believes that being single is the better state for you to be in, in order for him to bless you at the moment. 'There is no wisdom or understanding or counsel against the LORD.'[3] God calls singleness, among other things, a 'calling'[4] in which we should remain if we can, but he is realistic about the fact that most of us tend towards marriage as our preferred state.[5] The Lord is extremely positive about the benefits of remaining single, as 'he who is unmarried cares for the things of the Lord—how he may please the Lord. But he who is married cares about the things of the world—how he may please his wife.'[6] Whether you realize it or not, God wants to spare us pain and his greatest aim is our sanctification, to make us like Jesus.[7] If getting married will not help achieve this aim, God will not direct us that way, and will give us 'everything we need for life and godliness'[8] without a partner. If getting married is good for us, God will select the person, the timing and the way.

Highly value good Christian friendship

I'm convinced that much of the hankering after romantic relationships at all costs is down to the inability of modern Christians to forge strong friendships with those of the same gender: 'As iron sharpens iron, so a man sharpens the countenance of his friend.'[9] God says that it is not good for a man to be alone, but the solution to that problem does not always have to be one specific person of the opposite gender. We will not be married to each other in heaven[10] but will be worshipping the Lord all together as one body. There is great joy from Christian friendship and fellowship which is entirely forgotten because of our solitary pursuits (work, TV, computer games, gym, etc.) or because of our single-mindedness in trying to grab a partner for ourselves. 'Ointment and perfume delight the heart, and the sweetness of a man's friend gives delight by hearty counsel.'[11] You would think that 'perfume' goes with romance only, but the Bible speaks much more warmly of friendship than we do in our sex-obsessed culture. Friendships should be desirable, sweet-smelling things in our lives, just as much as romance.

Desire to present everyone perfect before Christ

We have spoken already of this, the highest possible motive and driving force in our Christian lives. The entire book of 1 Thessalonians shows how Paul's passion for seeing younger Christians built up and perfected in Jesus far outweighs that in most of the romances you will ever read about! A friend loves at all times,[12] and presenting someone perfect to Jesus is the most loving thing you can do for them.

Keep half an eye out for a potential Proverbs 31 wife/Ephesians 5 husband, while concentrating on being godly yourself

1 Corinthians 7:27 actually says that those who are single should not 'seek a wife', but Proverbs 18:22 says that 'He who finds a wife finds a good thing, and obtains favour from the LORD'. You know, it is possible to find something without really searching for it (this is why I say 'half an eye'). And often we find precious things when we are on the hunt for something else, don't we? We've all done it: we've found a beautiful old watch of our grandfather's while we were looking for our car keys, or something like that. And that truly is the Bible way: seek the Lord and his righteousness first, and he will make sure you 'obtain favour'. If you concentrate on delighting yourself in the Lord and seeking his bidding, he will give you the desires of your heart[13] without you really searching for them or even knowing perhaps quite what they were until they were fulfilled. It is more important that we pursue our own sanctification[14] in the Lord than that we pursue getting a partner. This way, we will be suitable marriage material if and when the Lord does finally send along the right person—much joy lies in this!

If you do find someone who loves the Lord, is single and is interested in you ...?

Praise the Lord! Maybe he is guiding you to marry; but be cautious, because although 'God made man upright, [we] have sought out many schemes'.[15] Pray daily that the Lord will confirm, delay or deny the answer, according to what is best for you both and what pleases him the most. 'He who guards his lips guards his life, but he who speaks rashly will come to ruin.'[16] Take counsel from your parents (particularly if they are believers)[17] and from a few trusted wiser Christians. Pray and talk seriously with your chosen partner about courtship, but don't speak of marriage too soon, in case you are not able to follow through your intentions; at the same time, don't fool around with someone's heart or 'play it casual'. How much wisdom from the Lord is required in this area on a daily basis! It is really important that you are both fully agreed on where you are heading with the Lord. Are you both able to attend the same church, for example, or is one of you a conservative and the other a charismatic? It's a pity that these issues need to be considered, but in far too many cases Christians actually attend different churches from their marriage partners, or one partner is dragged along to a church which they find very difficult. Some other Christian couples don't even pray or study the Bible together. This is a great shame because, of course, it means that you cannot have complete fellowship with the person you have complete intimacy with. You are one flesh in marriage, but not one mind in worship. You are walking parallel but separate paths to heaven. It also causes confusion for children and the church family as a whole. Spiritual like-mindedness must be the root of Christian marriage, not just a baseline, tick-the-Christian-box, minimal agreement. 'Can two walk together, unless they are agreed?'[18] The great delight of the lover in the Song of Solomon is that his spouse is also his sister, and this oneness must be our aim, too, in choosing a husband or wife.

Finally, let me ask just one question to those who think they have found their perfect Christian man or lady. Girls: Could you respect this man enough to submit yourself to his lead, as spiritual head of the relationship? And for boys: Could you honour this lady enough to self-sacrificially lay down your life for her?

Notes

1 Proverbs 16:3.

2 Matthew 25:21.

3 Proverbs 21:30.

4 1 Corinthians 7:20,24,27.

5 1 Corinthians 7:1–9; Matthew 19:12 says that if we can accept singleness, we should accept it, implying that it is truly an honoured state to be in—placing us in one sense alongside John the Baptist, Paul and even the Lord Jesus himself.

6 1 Corinthians 7:33.

7 Romans 8:29.

8 2 Peter 1:3 (NIV).

9 Proverbs 27:17.

10 Matthew 22:30.

11 Proverbs 27:9. Proverbs 27 is a good friendship chapter!

12 Proverbs 17:17.

13 Psalm 37:3–6.

14 1 Thessalonians 4:1–8.

15 Ecclesiastes 7:29.

16 Proverbs 13:3 (NIV).

17 See Appendix A: Some thoughts for Christian parents.

18 Amos 3:3.

A final word

So, then, I wish you well in your walk with the Lord. If you have struggles in this area, as I have had, please don't hesitate to talk to a Christian you can trust, someone who will pray with you and for you, and who will be able to study the Bible with you. You are welcome to contact me via the publisher if there is any way I can help you out or pray for you.

Thanks be to God for all his kind gifts to us, especially his Son.

'Now may the God of peace himself sanctify you completely; and may your whole spirit, soul, and body be preserved blameless at the coming of our Lord Jesus Christ. He who calls you is faithful, who also will do it' (1 Thessalonians 5:23–24).

Amen!

STOP AND PRAISE

Some thoughts for Christian parents

In modern society, parents seem to have no role at all in guiding their children in relationship and marriage choices. Any advice they give is often either politely ignored or actively resented. But in the Bible, they clearly have a big role, so if you are a Christian parent, do not feel you have no part to play!

Throughout the Old Testament, parents had a great deal of input into who their children married, and this seems to be the way that the Lord designed it. Isaac married Rebekah, who was selected by his father from among those who worshipped the same true God, and their marriage was a great success, being the only monogamous one among the patriarchs. In turn, Isaac advised his son Jacob not to 'take a wife from the daughters of Canaan'.[1] But his son Esau refused to accept advice from his parents and married two pagan women who 'were a grief of mind to Isaac and Rebekah'[2] because the parents knew that the wives would steal their son away from the Lord.

Deuteronomy 22 is a helpful chapter to read on this subject of parental involvement. Fathers and mothers are encouraged to:

• Safeguard and defend the chastity of their virgin children, particularly daughters (v. 15).

• Give their children away in marriage, particularly daughters (v. 16); even today in most wedding ceremonies, fathers 'give their daughters away'. This should signify something, and should at least mean that the father does have a right to be involved with his daughter's choice. In verse 28, where a girl has sex before marriage with a man, they are robbing the father of his parental responsibility. Hence, in verse 29, the man who has taken the girl without permission must pay the father fifty shekels of silver to compensate. That is an incredible amount of money: Patriarch.com[3] says that it equates to about $110,000 or eleven years' labour! Even under normal circumstances, a bridal price quite often had to be paid to the father, as in the seven years' labour Jacob paid to Laban for Rachel, or the 100 Philistine warriors killed by David to pay Saul for Michal.

Children nowadays are conditioned by society to believe that 'it's my body and I can do what I like with it', even to the extent of killing another human who is within their body, as with abortion. In May 2004, a British school even assisted a fourteen-year-old girl to have an abortion without her parents' knowledge. Our culture of individualism, selfishness and death will continue to slide into godless oblivion, but we as believers must continue to stand by God's Word and follow its precepts: 'Your word I have hidden in my heart, that I might not sin against you.'[4]

So, sadly, any parent of teenage or young adult children will have to face this clash of biblical values (i.e. chastity, restraint, parental involvement, godly courtship, marriage) with the world's values (i.e. promiscuity, excess, parental exclusion, godless relationships, serial monogamy).

Sociologists refer to the family as 'primary socialization' and peers, school, the media, etc. as 'secondary socialization'. This is why it's so important that Christian parents instil godly values in the area of relationships early on: 'Train up [or start] a child in the way he should go, and when he is old he will not depart from it.'[5] Even children from non-Christian backgrounds can understand good reasoning when it is presented to them with compassion and understanding. How much more should children of Christian backgrounds, by grace and the Holy Spirit's help, be able to be trained in godly standards early on, so that when they reach their teens they are prepared for the onslaught of the world's 'secondary socialization', and are ready to combat it with Scripture verses, prayer and consultation with their parents.

Having said this, I do not want to create a feeling of failure in any Christian parents who have children who are unconverted or have started 'seeing' unbelievers. We are saved by God's sovereign choice, and the best parents in the world cannot guarantee the salvation of their offspring: consider Isaac (son: Esau), Samuel (Joel and Abijah)[6] and Hezekiah (Manasseh). At the same time, God can, and does, save people from the most unbelievably evil backgrounds: think of good King Josiah and his wicked father Amon, for example.

The point is, then, that a godly upbringing, scriptural teaching from an early age on the subject of relationships, a culture of openness and honesty, and a freedom to express doubts, fears, failures and longings are all incredibly valuable in steering children into a godly future, especially with regard to their marriage choices. My parents brought me up to fear the Lord and walk in his ways, and despite major excursions into the world, through their prayers and admonition the Lord brought me back into the old paths that they had always said I should walk in. Therefore do not despair if your children are currently far from the Lord. The story is not over yet: remember that the fervent prayers of a righteous mum and dad avail much![7]

A big dilemma for a lot of parents is this: 'What if I lose my child's affection through challenging him on this? If I "interfere" with his choice of girlfriend, he may stop speaking to me!' This is a very real worry. Parents and others often silently watch their children and friends courting disaster, simply because they do not want to risk the precious relationships they have with them. They have so much to lose, it seems, by bringing a negative component into the mix. Very quickly they will be seen as a *persona non grata* and a killjoy, and be locked out of every aspect of their child/friend's life, not just out of the relationship arena.

I have experienced this alienation on numerous occasions myself, from both sides of the coin. I used to 'see' non-Christians, had parents and Christian friends rebuke me, and became alienated from them. I praise God that they cared more about my soul than about keeping the peace between us, or their own self-image as 'nice, non-judgemental people'. They risked my anger and the loss of the relationship, but they saved my life. On the other hand, I have lost around a dozen friends through their marriages/long-term relationships with non-Christians because in the end it came down to this: 'You can only be my friend if you endorse or at least remain silent about this ungodly relationship.'

One mother I knew saw her daughter about to marry an unbeliever and said to me that she did not want to lose her daughter's love, and so wasn't going to stand against it in any way. But this cannot be right. The Lord and his Word, and that person's soul must come above our own sense of discomfort, embarrassment or fear of losing affection or of being perceived as judgemental. Would any of the prophets have ever said any of God's words if they felt this way? Would anybody ever preach the good news of the Lord Jesus Christ if their dominating thought was whether people would reject them or not? Would Jesus have ever come to this earth if his big question was whether he would be accepted or not?[8] No, '"whatever I command you, you shall speak. Do not be afraid of their faces, for I am with you to deliver you," says the LORD.'[9] Fear of man brings a snare,[10] both to us and to those whom we fear losing. Through our selfish desire always to 'be the good guy', it may well be that that person walks away from the Lord completely.

Instead, if you love your child, lovingly warn him; open rebuke is better than hidden love,[11] and whoever 'turns a sinner from the error of his way will save [him] from death and cover a multitude of sins'.[12]

I'd like to present a few specific scenarios here which may apply to you.

Christian father and mother with an unbelieving child who is (considering) going out with an unbeliever

Obviously, in all these cases, the circumstances of the child (i.e. whether living at the family home or not) will affect the situation. We have biblical precedent in that Isaac was still living with Abraham (father selected bride), whereas Jacob was not living with Isaac (son selected bride, but still from believing 'stock'). Also, the age of the child is significant: if he is under eighteen, parental consent for marriage must, by law, be given (an interesting affirmation of scriptural values in itself). In Mississippi, parental consent is needed if either the fiancé or his bride-to-be is under twenty-one, but with that consent girls can marry at the age of fifteen! UK society sees the 'age of consent' as the important thing, but perhaps the model of some American states is closer to the Scriptures in that 'parental consent' is the critical value.[13] This would no doubt be borne out by most cultures in most of history, not least the Jewish culture even to this day.

But, in practice, most unbelieving children who are heading down the dating path are not initially interested in marriage, so the battleground will be fought on whether they should be going out day and night with Billy X or Jessica Y. However, the number one issue in your child's life is that he needs to come to the Lord in repentance and faith, not that he needs to stop dating. It makes sense that if his heart is with the world, he will seek out this world's patterns of behaviour, including dating. So the challenge for parents in this situation is to talk more about the Lord Jesus Christ and what your child thinks of him, rather than have a big argument about why you think such-and-such a girlfriend is unsuitable. It was only after hearing and being convicted by the Word of God that the people of Israel returned to the Lord in Ezra's day. And only then did they weep 'very bitterly' and confess their sins: 'We have trespassed against our God, and have taken pagan wives from the peoples of the land; yet now there is hope in Israel in spite of this. Now therefore, let us make a covenant with our God to put away all these wives ...'[14]

Christian father and mother with a believing child who is (considering) going out with an unbeliever

This is similar to the first scenario in that, even if your child is a genuine believer, he may well have rebelled against the Lord in this fundamental area of his life. So, first of all, I would offer to pray with him about his relationship with the Lord Jesus Christ, before even getting on to the subject of the dating, which here is, after all, just a symptom of becoming distant from the Lord. Solomon would never have married all those pagan women if he had been walking close to the Lord at the time.

If your child is willing to listen and sincere about following Jesus, then hopefully many of the arguments from the Word of God in this book can be rephrased and applied to help him see that the Lord is *for* him and seeks his blessing rather than his destruction: 'And you know in all your hearts and in all your souls that not one thing has failed of all the good things which the LORD your God spoke concerning you. All have come to pass for you; not one word of them has failed.'[15] And the Lord has set down in his Word the fact that blessing comes through obedience to his commands, including that which forbids being unequally yoked together with unbelievers. You can simply ask your child whether he loves Jesus and wants to keep his commandments. The arguments that come back at you might be along the lines of:

- 'She will become a Christian before the summer, I can promise you that.'[16]
- 'Don't worry, Mum, it's not like we're going to get married or anything.'
- 'Seriously, thanks Dad, but I don't think it's any of your business.'

Again, I hope that there are enough scriptural thoughts within this book to help answer these concerns, but sometimes there does come a limit as to how much one can usefully say: 'A wise son heeds his father's instruction, but a scoffer does not listen to rebuke.'[17] Then parents must devote themselves to prayer, as a far more effective activity than argument, and believe that the Lord who led your child to faith in the first place will lead him to repent of this folly also.

Christian father and mother with a believing child who is (considering) going out with a believer

Encourage your child to think carefully through what the Bible says about relationships and marriage (Chapter 6), recommend good books such as *I Kissed Dating Goodbye* and *Boy Meets Girl* by Josh Harris, pray with him for wisdom and guidance, and create a welcoming atmosphere at home where the courtship can be played out safely and with godly boundaries. Whether or not you particularly like the prospective partner, you should welcome her in the Lord because the key question is whether she will be a spiritual asset to your child, one who can help him grow to become more like the Lord Jesus Christ, to whose image we are all being conformed.[18]

One problem that can arise here is that often a professing believer is not the same as a genuine believer, and I know of several cases where parents have worried about their child's choice of partner, because, although nominally a Christian, she showed very few marks of grace. This requires very delicate handling and much wisdom, but I would urge you to remember once again that the wounds of a friend are better than the kisses of an enemy.[19] Speak now, because otherwise they will have too much time after their marriage for regrets and to question why you never warned them: 'He who spares his rod hates his son, but he who loves him, disciplines him promptly.'[20]

Christian parent with unbelieving spouse and believing child who is (considering) going out with an unbeliever

Jesus said, 'Do not think that I came to bring peace on earth. I did not come to bring peace, but a sword. For I have come to set "a man against his father, a daughter against her mother, and a daughter-in-law against her mother-in-law."'[21] It is a painful fact that many families are split in two with one spouse attending church with one child, and the other spouse and child remaining at home. However, in many ways this family is blessed, despite appearances! For one thing, 'The unbelieving husband is sanctified by the wife, and the unbelieving wife is sanctified by the husband; otherwise your children would be unclean, but now they are holy.'[22] This is hard to understand fully, but the Holy Spirit absolutely affirms fidelity in existing marriage relationships, and that even unbelieving parties benefit through this. And the reality is that the children do get far more biblical input than they would have had if both their parents were unbelievers, and from my observation, women who have become converted after marriage exert a greater (spiritual) influence on their children than do their unbelieving husbands, for example.

Also, we are told in 1Peter 3:1–2 that believing wives have strong grounds for hope, that they may win over their husbands to Christ by their godly conduct. But until that point, it can be difficult to give godly counsel to a believing child who might perhaps be tempted to play one parent off against the other, especially when he knows that the unbelieving parent is more likely to give him the green light for whatever he does. This can make you, the believing parent, feel quite lonely; you are trying to guide your child to cultivate godly relationships, and you have no back-up from your spouse in this. And your child can always turn around and say, for example, 'Well, look at you and Mum. She's not a Christian, and you're happily married.' But here you can point out the tremendous burden that you have for your not-yet-converted spouse, and that married life to an unbeliever is incredibly hard and not to be recommended, though God in his grace often works wonders after the event. If you are in this situation, you have my warmest encouragements to persevere, because your labour for the Lord is never in vain,[23] and if God is for you, who can be against you?[24]

Notes

1 Genesis 28:1.

2 Genesis 26:35.

3 http://www.patriarch.com/cov&inher.html

4 Psalm 119:11.

5 Proverbs 22:6.

6 1 Samuel 8:1–5.

7 James 5:16.

8 John 1:11.

9 Jeremiah 1:7–8.

10 Proverbs 29:25.

11 Proverbs 27:5.

12 James 5:20.

13 http://usmarriagelaws.com/search/united_states/teen_marriage_laws/index.shtml

14 Ezra 10:1–3.

15 Joshua 23:14.

16 Someone actually said something like this to me.

17 Proverbs 13:1; compare with 9:8.

18 Romans 8:29.

19 Proverbs 27:6.

20 Proverbs 13:24.

21 Matthew 10:34–35.

22 1 Corinthians 7:14.

Appendix A

23 1 Corinthians 15:58.

24 Romans 8:31.

Some thoughts on ethnic issues

Cross-cultural marriage

Ken Ham, in his superb talks on Creation, often touches on the subject of racial origins. He maintains, quite irrefutably, that we all come from one man (Adam) and therefore are all of the same race (fallen humans!). He says that, nevertheless, there is another 'race' of humans, that is, those who are in the second Adam, Christ.[1] He expresses his dismay that some Christian parents would be more upset if their daughter brought home someone with a different skin colour, than they would be if she brought home an unbeliever. A black believer and a white believer are absolutely entitled to marry before the Lord, infinitely more so than, for example, a white unbeliever and a white believer. Ham points out that we all have the same pigment in our skins (melanin), and we are all the same colour, just varying shades of it.

So the first point is that there is nothing biblical that prevents people of different ethnicities from marrying, providing they both love the Lord. However, there are always hurdles in relationships, such as geographical distance, differences in habits, temperaments, tastes in music and food, how you get on with each other's family, etc., as we all know! And ethnicity is another dimension to be considered when marrying someone: you can't just say, 'Oh well, the Holy Spirit will smooth out any problems.' Jesus says, 'Suppose one of you wants to build a tower. Will he not first sit down and estimate the cost to see if he has enough money to complete it?'[2] In the same way, you have to think through carefully which country you are going to live in; if you will have children, what languages they will learn; how you are going to order your house, and so on. I don't think we can just shrug our shoulders at these things, but at the same time, none of them should present insuperable barriers if the Lord is in it![3]

Pressure to marry within one's ethnic community

When someone crosses over from death to life, repents and accepts Jesus Christ as Lord and Saviour, a wonderful new birth has taken place! On the inside, there is a new creation. On the outside, however, things look the same. Imagine a Hindu man comes to Christ in Uttar Pradesh in northern India. He looks the same as he ever did, but there is a joy and a peace within that nothing can destroy, as he has come to know the Saviour of the world. He hasn't told his family yet, and is looking for an opportunity to break it to them, when his father announces he has found a wife for him. The poor new believer knows that this girl is very unlikely to be a Christian, and he has the massive dilemma of offsetting the fifth Commandment (honour your parents) against the first (worship no God before me). He knows that if he marries a Hindu girl, he will be torn away from worshipping Jesus with all his heart, mind, soul and strength.

The key here would seem to be to decide which Commandment takes precedence. And it is surely no accident that the first Commandment holds the position that it does. Jesus sums up the law in, firstly, loving God, and, secondly, loving your neighbour. So if loving God and loving your neighbour (or family) appear to conflict, God must come first. This is why Jesus says, 'If anyone comes to me and does not hate his father and mother, wife and children, brothers and sisters, yes, even his own life also, he cannot be my disciple.'[4]

In any case, we love our neighbours and family by loving God. Even if we appear to go against their wishes, we are giving them a godly witness of who God is, how precious his laws are, what his character is like (he does not mix light with darkness). We are actually blessing them far more than if we just went along with them. And even if the new believer's life is in danger, as Jesus says, we must love God more than our lives. Now this is very easy for me to say as a Western male of independent circumstances, and perhaps all of us in the family of God in the West need to take a long, hard look at our failure to pray deeply and often for the plight of our brothers and sisters in these impossible dilemmas. Impossible, that is, without the grace of God, who delights in performing what we ourselves cannot do.

Notes

1 See Romans 5 and 1 Corinthians 15.

2 Luke 14:28 (NIV).

3 Psalm 127:1.

4 Luke 14:26.

A summary of the key points

Should Christians date non-Christians?

1. Necessary attitudes

We need to:
1. Want to please God (John 14:15; Luke 6:46; Hebrews 11:6).
2. Believe that the Bible is God's perfect and sufficient Word (2 Timothy 3:14–17).
3. Believe that God has our best interests at heart (Psalm 34:8,10; 84:11).
4. Pray for the Spirit to guide us through God's Word (Psalm 119:18; John 16:13).

2. Reasons not to go out with a non-Christian

It is wrong to go out with/marry a non-Christian because …
The Bible says NO (*2 Corinthians 6:14–18;* 1 Corinthians 7:39b; 9:5; Numbers 25; Deuteronomy 7:3–4; 1 Kings 11:1–10; Ezra 10; Nehemiah 13:10–31). This is because:
1. Believers and unbelievers are *unequally yoked,* i.e. totally unsuited to walking through life together, aiming for completely different goals (Amos 3:3).
2. Believers are righteous and in the *light*, unbelievers are lawless and in the *dark* (John 3:19–21).
3. Believers are the temple of God which belongs to *Christ,* and unbelievers are idolaters, following after the *devil* (Ephesians 2:1–6).
4. Believers must *separate themselves* from unbelievers if they want God to receive them as their Father (1 John 2:15).
If you think 2 & 3 sound particularly strong, remember that this is what God himself says in his Word. Believers and unbelievers can seem indistinguishable at times. Believers can appear very unrighteous and darkened in their mind and behaviour, and unbelievers can seem very kind and nice, but, fundamentally, every true believer is *in Christ,* and he is the only true light of the World. Every unbeliever *rejects Christ,* and so (usually without realizing it) is still following the devil's path to destruction.
There is only *one main reason* not to go out with non-Christians because …
                            … we should need *no stronger reason than God's Word*!

3. Motives & self-justification

Examine your motives! Are you justifying yourself?
Dating for fun? Is it OK just to go out or see each other, as long as it's nothing serious?

No, because the purpose of courtship is engagement, nothing else. Otherwise it leads to:
1. Heartache (Proverbs 26:18–19).
2. Heading away from making God's kingdom our priority (Matthew 6:33).
3. Harming future relationships (Hosea 8:7).
Evangelistic dating? Is it OK to go out with someone in order to try to convert them? No, it is unkind and unloving because going out with an unbeliever...
1. Pleases the devil who is seeking to trick believers into ungodly relationships; I believe it is his number one tactic for new believers (1 Peter 5:8; Galatians 3:1).
2. Pours scorn on the Bible, which is the only light to our path (Psalm 119:105).
3. Places both of you in danger—it's spiritually and sexually highly toxic (1 Corinthians 15:33–34; Joshua 23:12–13).

4. Eternal consequences

For the Christian:
1. Our works will be burnt up and we will suffer loss.
2. The blood of the unbeliever will be on our hands.
For the non-Christian—the danger of perishing in sin and going to hell.

5. Some common objections

'I know a Christian couple and one of them wasn't a Christian when they first started going out.'
This is extremely rare. And even when it does happen, we must remember that just because God is gracious, this is not an encouragement to sin. And finally, these couples would want you to follow their advice, not their example. They would say, 'Steer well clear.'

6. Positive alternatives (from Proverbs!)

1. Commit your works to the Lord, and your thoughts will be established (Proverbs 16:3).
2. Be prepared to accept that God knows better than you do (Proverbs 21:30).
3. Highly value good Christian friendship (Proverbs 27:9,17).
4. Desire to love everyone purely and present them perfect before Christ (Proverbs 17:17).
5. Keep half an eye out for a godly future husband/wife, while seeking godliness yourself (Proverbs 18:22; 31).
6. If you do find someone who loves the Lord, is single and is interested in you ...? (Amos 3:3).

No Longer Two

A guide to Christian marriage preparation

Brian and Barbara Edwards
Large format paperback, 144 pages,
ISBN 1 903087 00 7

With more than one in three marriages ending in divorce, this God-ordained relationship is more under threat than ever and divorce among Christians is at an all-time high. In response to this, churches now offer pre-marital counselling for engaged couples. Some clergy now refuse to marry a couple unless they have taken such a course. *No Longer Two* is a highly acclaimed marriage preparation guide offering an exciting way of working together to build a strong marriage based upon the clear teaching and common sense of the Bible. Whether or not you are familiar with the Bible, you will find this an easy-to-use guide—perfect for individuals and groups alike. Includes Bible studies to ensure that the reader actually gets involved in finding out what Scripture has to say about the subject.

Quite simply one of the best books on the market today on the subject of marriage—*The Monthly Record*

What the Bible says about going out, marriage and sex

Chris Richards and Liz Jones
Illustrated booklet, 64 pages
ISBN 1 903087 87 2

G od calls us to follow him in every area of our lives, and one of the most challenging is in the realm of our sexuality. We were beautifully, intricately created as sexual beings, but we are so quickly marred when we disregard God's instructions. Here, two doctors sensitively address the matter within a clear biblical and medical framework.

Dr Chris Richards and Dr Liz Jones are medical doctors working from the north of England. They are presenters and trustees for the charity 'Lovewise'.

- Topical issue addressed within clear biblical and common sense framework
- Part of a new series of 'Wise Choices' booklets based on Proverbs 4:5–7
- Includes Bible reference section to provide key teaching from the Scriptures
- Uses engaging and symbolic illustrations

'... Honestly and frankly explains what the Bible teaches on sex and relationships.'—Roger Carswell

'... Straight, honest answers'—Sharon James

'This is a fantastic booklet, aimed primarily at Christian young people ... It is certainly the most concise and honest book I have ever read on the subject.'—*Evangelical Times*

Notes

Notes